# My Beautiful, Broken Shell

---

*Discovering Beauty
In Our Brokenness*

---

Blessings
and love,
Carol Hamblet Adams

# My Beautiful, Broken Shell

*Discovering Beauty In Our Brokenness*

*by*
Carol Hamblet Adams

*Illustrated by*
Bobbie Wilkinson

*Eagle Press*
Attleboro, MA

# *My Beautiful, Broken Shell*

## Discovering Beauty In Our Brokenness

*by*

Carol Hamblet Adams

Published by:

**Eagle Press**
Post Office Box 1149
Attleboro, MA 02703-0020

Copyright © 1996 by Carol Hamblet Adams
First Printing 1997
Second Printing 1997
Printed in the United States of America
Illustrations © 1996 by Bobbie Wilkinson
Graphic Design by Custom Graphics,
   Paeonian Springs, VA

Publisher's Cataloging in Publication

Adams, Carol Hamblet
   My beautiful, broken shell: discovering beauty in our brokenness / by Carol Hamblet Adams ; illustrated by Bobbie Wilkinson.
   p. cm.
   Preassigned LCCN: 96-90770
   ISBN 0-9655088-5-4

   1. Self-acceptance. 2. Self-esteem. 3. Pain.
   I. Wilkinson, Bobbie. II. Title.

BF575.S37A43 1997               158.1

# This Book Belongs To:

# *Preface*

This book began in 1982, shortly after my husband, Steve, was diagnosed with multiple sclerosis. I was feeling frightened... discouraged...alone.

I went to the beach one day and decided to gather a few shells for my collection. The first one I picked up was a broken scallop shell, so I threw it back. But then I picked it up again and saw myself as I was at that moment...broken, too...just like the shell. God spoke to me about my brokenness, and I put His words on paper.

Over the years, this reflection has helped me and many others get through difficult times. I have published this with the hope that it will help you or someone you love...that you may find comfort in the gentle words...in the beautiful illustrations...and that, through this book, you will find hope.

My deepest wish is that you always know how truly beautiful you are...not <u>despite</u> your brokenness...but <u>because</u> of it.

With my love and prayers,

*Carol*

# Acknowledgements

*To* Linda Blackman, my good friend and first mentor, for believing in me...

*To* my colleagues in the National Speakers Association and New England Speakers Association for your constant friendship, advice and support...

*To* my relatives and friends who have stood by me over the years and given me unfailing love and encouragement...

*To* the many who were strong enough to share their brokenness with me...

*To* Bob and Linda Farkas of Custom Graphics, whose combined talents as artists and consultants helped pull this book together. You were an absolute joy to work with...

*To* Bobbie Wilkinson, my partner and collaborator...for your tireless efforts...for all the laughs...for your exquisite illustrations that gave sight to my words...and especially for sharing my dream...

*And* to the Lord, for His inspiration and guidance...

*Thank you all for making this book possible.*

# Dedication

*To* Mom and Dad, for giving me life, love, and my greatest gift, my faith...

*To* my husband, Steve, for sharing my life...for your inspiration, love, and total support of all my dreams...

*To* Todd, Kevin and Kristin, my greatest treasures, for making me the proudest and luckiest Mom in the world...

*And* in loving memory of Emily and Rog Adams, two of my life's richest blessings.

*The Lord is close to the brokenhearted; and those who are crushed in spirit He saves.*

– Psalms 34:19

# My Beautiful, Broken Shell

*D*awn has broken
on a beautiful day here
at the ocean. I've
come to refresh my
weary spirit and to
refuel my tired soul.

$\mathcal{I}$'m so grateful for
the peace and the calm
of the seashore,
where time stands
still and unrushed...

...where I can see and
feel the beauty
all around me.

This is my first
morning at the ocean,
and as I walk to the beach,
feeling the rich, warm
sand beneath my feet,

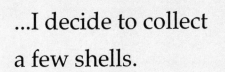

...I decide to collect
a few shells.

*I*t is low tide and
I watch, mesmerized,
as the ocean rises slowly...
curls...

...and then spills
its white-laced foam
onto the shore.

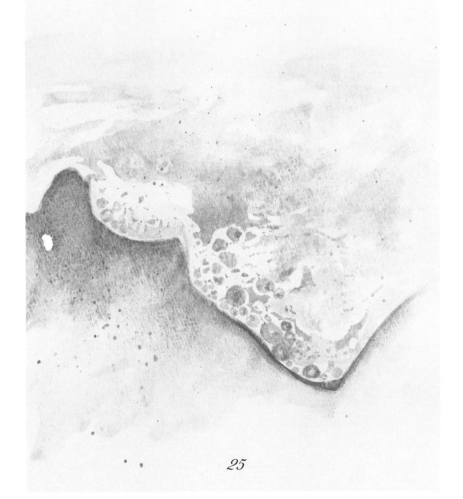

$\mathcal{I}$walk by a
broken scallop shell...

...and leave it to search
for more perfect ones.

*B*ut then I stop...
go back...and pick up
the broken shell.

$\mathcal{I}$ realize that this
shell is me with my
broken heart.

*T*his shell is people
who are hurting...
people who have lost
loved ones...

...people who are
frightened or alone...
people with
unfulfilled dreams.

This shell has had
to fight so hard to
keep from being
totally crushed by the
pounding surf...
just as I have had to...

...yet it is still
out on the beautiful,
sandy shore...
just as I am.

*"Thank You, Lord, that I haven't been completely crushed by the heaviness in my heart...*

*...by the pounding
of the surf."*

*I*f our world were
only filled with
perfect shells, we
would never learn
from adversity...
from pain...
from sorrow.

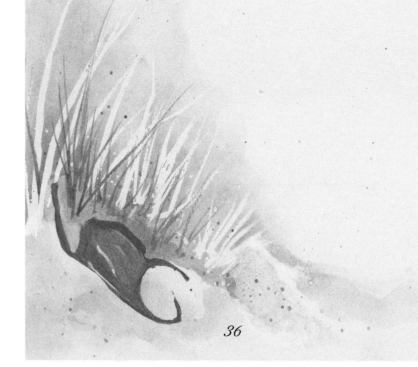

*W*e would miss
some of life's most
important lessons
along the way.

*"Thank You, Lord, for
all that I learn from
my brokenness...
for the courage it takes
to live amidst my pain...*

*...and for the
strength it takes
to remain
on the shore."*

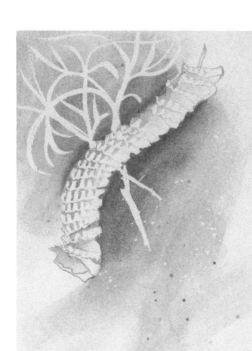

$\mathcal{B}$roken shells
teach us not to
look at our
imperfections...

...but to look at
the beauty...the
great beauty...
of what is still left.

*I*f anything is still left
of me or my loved ones,
then that is enough to
grab hold of...

...to thank God for...
to go on with.

*B*roken shells
mean lots of tears...
lots of pain...
lots of struggle...

...but broken shells
are also valuable tools
to teach faith, courage
and strength.

*B*roken shells inspire
others and demonstrate
the will to go on
in a way that no perfect
shell could ever do.

*B*roken shells are shells that have been tested...and tried... and hurt...yet they don't quit. They continue to be.

*"Thank You, Lord, for
the great strength
it takes to simply be...*

*...even when I hurt
so deeply that there
seems to be nothing
left of me."*

*As* I walk along the
beach picking up shells,
I  see that each one has
its own special beauty...
its own unique pattern.

*"Lord, help me see my*
*own, beautiful pattern...*
*and to remember that*
*each line and each color*
*on my shell was put there*
*by You."*

"Help me not compare
myself to others, so
that I  may appreciate
my own uniqueness."

*"Help me truly accept
myself just as I am,
so that I  may sing the
song in my heart...
for no one else has my
song to sing...my gift
to give."*

*I* watch the rolling surf toss new shells onto the shore, and I am reminded of the many times that I, too, have been tossed by the storms of life...

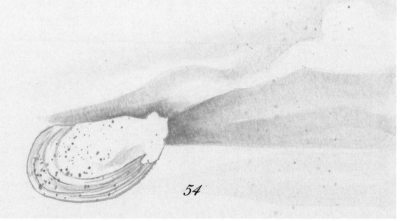

...and worn down by
the sands of time,
just like my beautiful,
broken shell.

*B*ut I am reminded
that broken shells
don't stand alone.
In our brokenness,
we still have the Lord.

*"Thank You, Lord, for
being with me
to share my life...
to help carry my
burdens."*

*"Thank You for the
precious gift of faith
that keeps me  strong,
when I am weak...
that keeps me going on,
when it would be
easier to quit."*

*"Thank You, Lord for hope in times of despair... for light in times of darkness...for patience in times of suffering...for assuring me that with You all things are possible."*

*A* wave crashes,
sending tiny sand crabs
scurrying for safety...
and I am reminded
that even the smallest
creatures depend on
each other.

$\mathcal{E}$specially in our brokenness, we need the Lord... and we need one another.

*"Thank You, Lord, for filling my life with people who care."*

*"Thank You for my family...for my friends... for those who are always there for me."*

$\mathcal{A}$s I look at my
beautiful, broken shell,
I see that it has
nothing to hide. It
doesn't pretend to be
perfect or whole...

...Its brokenness is clear
for everyone to see.

*"Lord, may I be*
*strong enough to show*
*my pain and brokenness*
*like this shell.*
*May I give myself*
*permission to hurt...*
*to cry...to be human."*

*"May I have the courage to
risk sharing my feelings
with others, so that I
may receive support
and encouragement along
the way."*

*"Lord, help me
reach out to others...
especially to the broken
and discouraged...
not only to love them...
but to learn from them
as well."*

*"May I listen...*
*comfort...*
*and give unconditional*
*love to all who pass*
*my way."*

*"Lord, help me
realize that I am not
the only one hurting...
that we all have pain
in our lives."*

*"Help me remember
that in my brokenness
I am still whole and
complete in Your sight."*

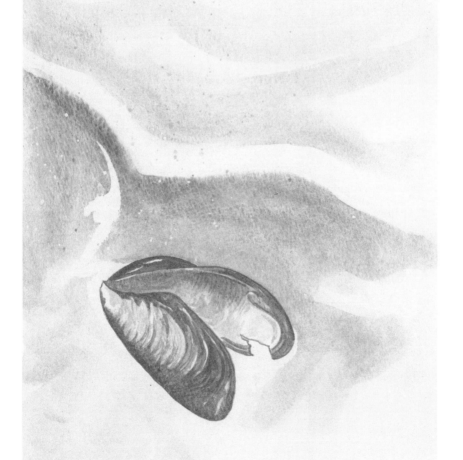

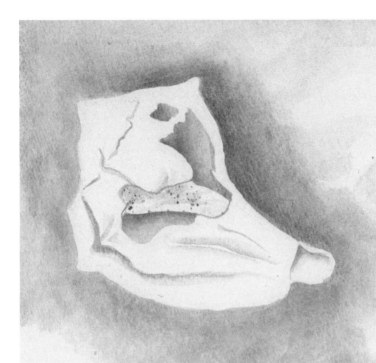

*I* walk amidst many
washed up shells, and
I suddenly spot a broken
conch shell...white and
ordinary on the outside...
yet a brilliant orange
inside.

*"Lord, help me see*
*through to the inside*
*of all people*
*who touch my life...*
*and to see everyone's*
*true colors."*

*H*ere at the beach,
I receive so many gifts.
I am grateful for
the inner peace that
fills my soul.

$\mathcal{S}$omehow, here at
the ocean, I take time
to notice sandpipers
playing along the shore...

...beach grasses swaying
in the salty breezes.

*I* delight in finding
simple treasures...
a piece of smooth,
green seaglass...
a transparent, white
stone...

...a starfish.

*"Lord, help me to*
*remain child-like*
*in my appreciation*
*of life."*

*"Please slow me down...*
*that I may always see*
*the extraordinary*
*in the ordinary."*

"May I always wonder
at a shell in the sand...
the dawn of a new day...
the beauty of a flower...

*...the blessing of a friend...*
*the love of a child."*

*"In my brokenness,
may I never take
life so seriously
that I fail to laugh
along the way."*

*"May I always take
the time to watch a kite
dance in the sky...
to sing...to pick daisies...
to love...to take risks...
to believe in my dreams."*

As I look once more
at the broken scallop
shell in my hand,
I am reminded of all
the beautiful shells
God has placed in
my midst.

"Lord, may I truly
appreciate every moment
spent with my loved ones
on Your earthly shores,
while this life is so
briefly mine."

*"Let me not destroy
the beauty of today
by grieving over
yesterday...or
worrying about
tomorrow."*

*"May I cherish and appreciate my shell collection to the fullest each and every day... for I know not when the tide will come and wash my treasures away."*

*"Thank You, Lord,
for embracing my shell...
whether I am whole
or broken."*

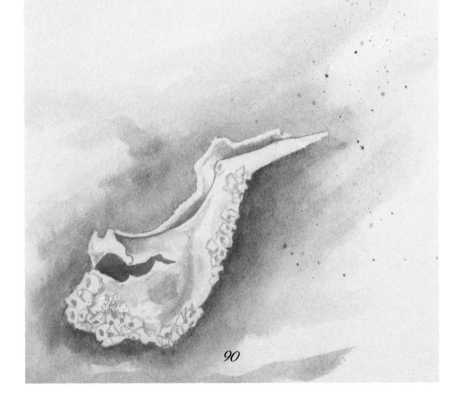

*"Thank You for sending
me loved ones who care."*

*"Thank You for
holding me in the
palm of Your hand...*

*...for keeping me safe
from the pounding surf."*

*A*nd now, I think
I'll continue walking
and add to my
beautiful collection
of shells.

# Afterword

Thank you for choosing this book for yourself or for someone you know. I hope that you have enjoyed reading *My Beautiful, Broken Shell* and that it has touched your heart. If you would like to share any of your thoughts with me, I would love to hear from you. I can be reached at:

 *Eagle Press*
Post Office Box 1149
Attleboro, MA 02703-0020

You may also contact me at the above address for information about speaking engagements or other programs and products.

God bless,

*Carol*

# Reflections

# Reflections

# *Order Form*

Please send _____ copy/copies of
*My Beautiful, Broken Shell* at $12.95 each to:

Name: _____

Address: _____

City: _____ State: ____ Zip: _____

Phone: ( _____ ) _____ - _____

**AMOUNT DUE:**

___ Copy/Copies at $12.95 ea.  $_____

MA residents add 5% sales tax    _____

Shipping & handling
   First book $3.00              _____

   Additional books add $.75 ea.  _____

**TOTAL ENCLOSED**        $ _____

Please make checks or money orders payable to:

*Eagle Press*
Post Office Box 1149
Attleboro, MA 02703-0020

Or call TOLL-FREE: 800-205-8254
Major Credit Cards Accepted

***Thank you very much for your order.***

# *Order Form*

Please send _____ copy/copies of
*My Beautiful, Broken Shell* at $12.95 each to:

Name: _____

Address: _____

City: _____ State: ____ Zip: _____

Phone: ( _____ ) _____ - _____

**AMOUNT DUE:**

___ Copy/Copies at $12.95 ea.  $_____

MA residents add 5% sales tax     _____

Shipping & handling
   First book $3.00                    _____

   Additional books add $.75 ea.  _____

**TOTAL ENCLOSED**          $ _____

Please make checks or money orders payable to:

 *Eagle Press*
Post Office Box 1149
Attleboro, MA 02703-0020

Or call TOLL-FREE: 800-205-8254
Major Credit Cards Accepted

*Thank you very much for your order.*

# *Order Form*

Please send _____ copy/copies of
*My Beautiful, Broken Shell* at $12.95 each to:

Name: _____

Address: _____

City: _____ State: _____ Zip: _____

Phone: ( _____ ) _____ - _____

**AMOUNT DUE:**

___ Copy/Copies at $12.95 ea.  $_____

MA residents add 5% sales tax    _____

Shipping & handling
  First book $3.00                _____

    Additional books add $.75 ea.  _____

**TOTAL ENCLOSED**        $  _____

Please make checks or money orders payable to:

*Eagle Press*
Post Office Box 1149
Attleboro, MA 02703-0020

Or call TOLL-FREE: 800-205-8254
Major Credit Cards Accepted

*Thank you very much for your order.*

## About the Author

Carol Hamblet Adams is a writer and motivational speaker, who has had a life-long love of the ocean. Carol gives keynote addresses to youth and adult audiences on subjects including self-esteem, keeping fun in your life and going for your dreams. She has worked for many years in education and does bereavement work, the topic of a forth-coming book. Carol is a member of the National Speakers Association and is a United States masters competitive swimmer. She enjoys acting, fishing, riding roller coasters, and singing with her twin sister, Bobbie Wilkinson. Carol and her husband, Steve, live in Massachusetts and have three children, Todd, Kevin and Kristin.

## About the Illustrator

Bobbie Wilkinson is a free-lance writer, artist, musician and songwriter, whose greatest joy has been raising her three daughters with her husband, Tom. "I lovingly dedicate these illustrations to Tom, Robyn, Kelly, and Brooke, who color my world with magic and merriment. . . and to the Lord, who guided my paintbrush on this project." Bobbie lives with her husband in a renovated barn in the northern Virginia countryside, where her favorite pastime is appreciating the beauty that surrounds her.